Studio Art Quilt Associates, Inc.
Portfolio 17
The art quilt sourcebook

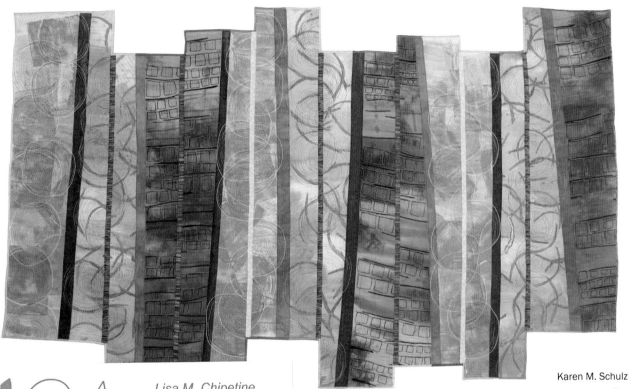

Karen M. Schulz

SAQA
Studio **Art** Quilt Associates

Lisa M. Chipetine
President
lchipetine@gmail.com

Please accept this copy of our latest publication, "Portfolio 17, The Art Quilt Sourcebook" with our compliments.

Lisa M. Chipetine

SAQA
Studio **Art** Quilt Associates

P.O. Box 572
Storrs, CT 06268-0572
USA
860-487-4199
www.SAQA.com • info@SAQA.com

Wendy Feldberg

Studio Art Quilt Associates, Inc. Portfolio 17

The Art Quilt Sourcebook

Published by Studio Art Quilt Associates, Inc.

All rights reserved.

Copyright © 2010 by Studio Art Quilt Associates, Inc.

Editor: Cheryl Dineen Ferrin

Book Design & Production: C. Dineen Ferrin Designs

ISBN-13: 978-0-9788853-7-3

ISBN-10: 0-9788853-7-6

Printed in the U.S.A.

Studio Art Quilt Associates, Inc.

P.O. Box 572, Storrs, Connecticut 06268-0572 USA

860-487-4199

www.SAQA.com ● info@SAQA.com

Front cover images
Top: Barbara Oliver Hartman
Bottom: Jo-Ann Golenia

Back cover image: Nelda Warkentin

Studio Art Quilt Associates, Inc.

Portfolio 17

The art quilt sourcebook

Linda W. Henke

Contents

Introduction

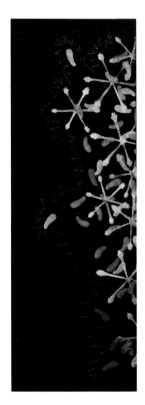 

Mary Vaneecke

Welcome to Studio Art Quilt Associates, Inc.'s new *Portfolio 17, The Art Quilt Sourcebook*. We hope that you will find this volume to be an exciting addition to your library.

We have added a number of interesting options to enhance your experience viewing the art quilts included in *Portfolio 17*. We now have a digital edition of the *Portfolio* at SAQA.com that allows you free, 24/7 access to the *Portfolio*. The digital edition includes a magnifying window that gives you a moveable, up-close view of any section of the pictured artwork. You can also search the digital edition for artists working in specific genres or geographical locations. Simply go to the menu bar, click "Find" and you are on your way.

We have also instituted a new searchable on-line database of Professional Artist Members who have been included in this and previous Portfolios.
In addition to being able to search by all the usual keywords, we have the artists categorized within the following genre:

Abstract	Color Work
Conceptual	Figurative
Nature	Representational
Sculptural	Still Life

For more detailed information or to download lists of artists who meet your desired criterion, please visit the SAQA website: www.saqa.com

We appreciate your interest in Studio Art Quilt Associates, and the many fine artists we represent.

The SAQA Board of Directors

Misik Kim

The Artists

Linda Abrams

I Dream of Africa
© 2008
32" x 21"
81 cm x 53 cm

Abstract

21 Robbins Lane
Lake Success, New York 11020

516-829-3859
info@lindasartisticadventures.com
www.lindasartisticadventures.com

Virginia Abrams

Reflections 4
© 2009
29" x 38"
74 cm x 97 cm

Nature

555 Holly Knoll Road
Hockessin, Delaware 19707

302-239-5110
GinnyAbrams@MSN.com
www.VirginiaAbrams.com

B.J. Adams

Nautical Narrative
© 2009
20" x 20"
51 cm x 51 cm

Still Life

2821 Arizona Terrace, N.W.
Washington, D.C. 20016

202-364-8404
bjfiber@aol.com
www.BJAdamsArt.com

Christine L. Adams

796 Nelson Street
Rockville, Maryland 20850

301-762-3267
uncommon.threads@erols.com
www.StoriesInFabric.com

Deidre Adams

Composition IX
© 2008
46" x 48"
117 cm x 122 cm

Abstract

614 Ridgemont Circle
Littleton, Colorado 80126

303-683-0316
deidre@deidreadams.com
www.deidreadams.com

Natalya Aikens

Piter 1
© 2009
18" x 18"
46 cm x 46 cm

Abstract

69 Ridgeview Drive
Pleasantville, New York 10570

917-414-7969
natalya@artbynatalya.com
www.artbynatalya.com

Frieda L. Anderson

Winter Forest
© 2008
27" x 35"
69 cm x 89 cm

Abstract

1995 Murcer Lane
Elgin, Illinois 60123

847-987-7556
quiltgoddess@gmail.com
www.friestyle.com

Ilse Anysas-Salkauskas

Order Out of Chaos
© 2008
45" x 30"
114 cm x 76 cm

Conceptual

P.O. Box 93
Cochrane, Alberta T4C 1A4
Canada

403-932-2284
ilse@anm.org
www.ilse.anm.org

Ludmila Aristova

The Alternation of Seasons/Summer
© 2009
27" x 14"
67 cm x 34 cm

Abstract

8020 Fourth Avenue, A6
Brooklyn, New York 11209

646-345-8777
Ludmila.Aristova@mac.com
www.ludmilaaristova.com

Jill Ault

Digits | 2531 Meade Court
© 2009 | Ann Arbor, Michigan 48105
40" x 40"
102 cm x 102 cm | 734-665-4601
| jillault@umich.edu
Abstract | www.jillault.com

Esterita Austin

Incommunicato
© 2009
54" x 54"
137 cm x 137 cm

Figurative

58 John Street
Port Jefferson Station, New York 11776

631-331-3429
esterita2@aol.com
www.esteritaaustin.com

Debbie Babin

Palm Island | 1111 Thompson Court
© 2009 | Saint Leonard, Maryland 20685
10" x 10"
25 cm x 25 cm | 410-586-3305
| debbiebabin@studioquilts.com
Nature | www.studioquilts.com

Teresa Barkley

Modern Antiquity
© 2009
20" x 20"
51 cm x 51 cm

Conceptual

9 Kensington Terrace
Maplewood, New Jersey 07040

973-830-7097
Quiltduck@gmail.com

Linda Beach

Map of Shadows
© 2008
39" x 54"
99 cm x 137 cm

Nature

22909 Green Garden Drive
Chugiak, Alaska 99567

907-688-3335
lbeach@gci.net
www.lindabeachartquilts.com

Alice M. Beasley

We Are a Nation
© 2009
37" x 42"
93 cm x 107 cm

Figurative

1018 Park Lane
Oakland, California 94610

510-465-6543
abeasley@sbcglobal.net
www.alicebeasley.com

Polly Bech

Another Spring Rain
© 2009
48" x 27"
122 cm x 69 cm

Nature

514 School Lane
Swarthmore, Pennsylvania 19081

610-543-3650
pbech@comcast.net
www.pollybech.com

Christi S. Beckmann

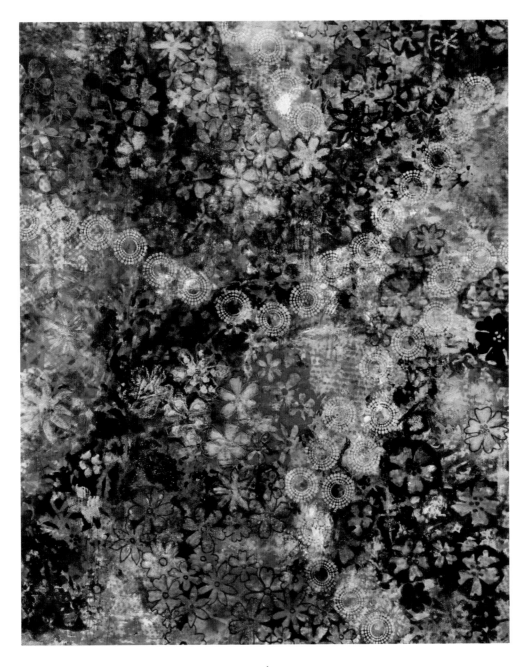

I Don't Care If You Don't
Like My Flower Garden
© 2009
39" x 32"
99 cm x 81 cm

Abstract

5519 Foothills Drive
Berthoud, Colorado 80513

970-532-7100
christibeckmann@yahoo.com
www.freereinarts.com

Sue A. Benner

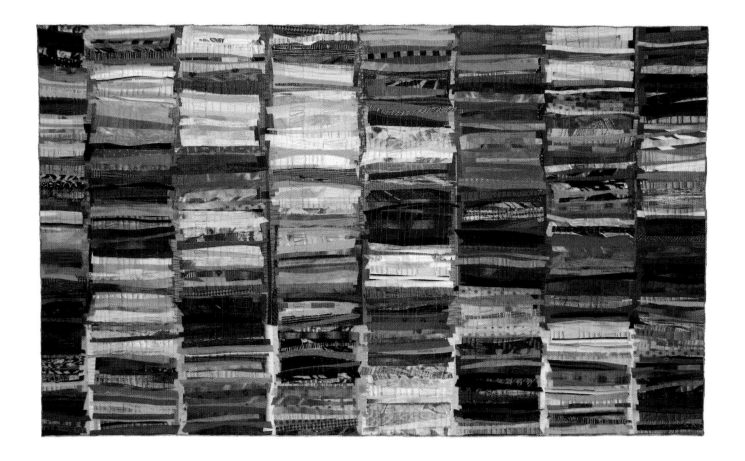

Display I
© 2008
30" x 50"
76 cm x 127 cm

Abstract

8517 San Fernando Way
Dallas, Texas 75218

214-796-8089
suebenner@aol.com
www.suebenner.com

Astrid Hilger Bennett

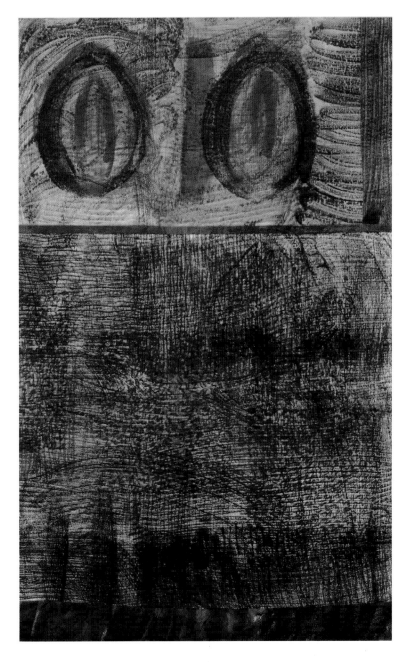

The Beauty of Innuendo
© 2010
60" x 38"
150 x cm x 95 cm

Abstract

909 Webster Street
Iowa City, Iowa 52240

319-430-3183
bennettic@mchsi.com
www.astridhilgerbennett.com

Regina V. Benson

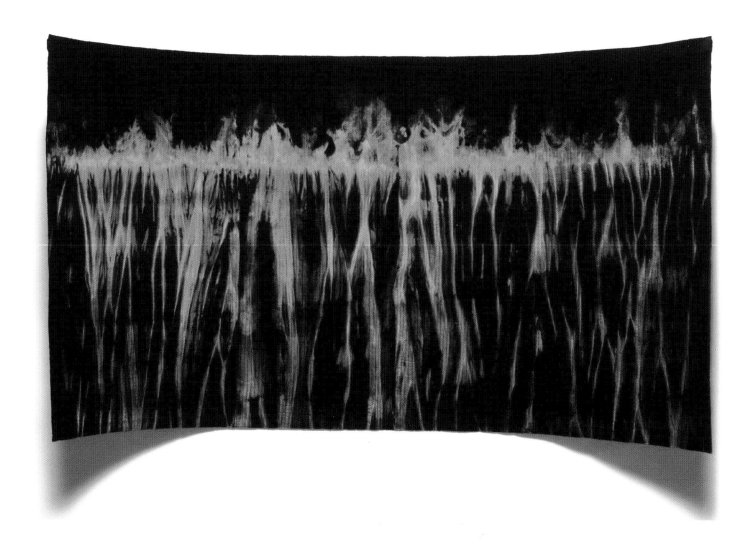

Ablaze | 14154 W. 1st Drive
© 2009 | Golden, Colorado 80401
38" x 62" |
97 cm x 158 cm | 303-278-0413
| regina-b@comcast.net
Nature | www.reginabenson.com

Charlotte S. Bird

Last Clear Chance
© 2009
38" x 38"
97 cm x 97 cm

Conceptual

2633 Reynard Way
San Diego, California 92103

619-294-7236
cbird2400@aol.com
www.birdworks-fiberarts.com

Eszter Bornemisza

Haiku
© 2008
37" x 37"
96 cm x 96 cm

Conceptual

Varosmajor u. 52.
Budapest, 01122
Hungary

36 30 3995728
eszter@bornemisza.com
www.bornemisza.com

Ann Brauer

Autumn Afternoon
© 2008
45" x 45"
114 cm x 114 cm

Abstract

2 Conway Street
Shelburne Falls, Massachusetts 01370

413-625-8605
ann@annbrauer.com
www.annbrauer.com

Melani K. Brewer

Merlin the Great Horned Owl
© 2008
30" x 22"
76 cm x 56 cm

Nature

3801 Bridge Road
Cooper City, Florida 33026

954-431-8700
melanibrewerstudio@att.net
www.melanibrewer.com

Eliza Brewster

Prime Meats
© 2009
40" x 37"
102 cm x 94 cm

Conceptual

1991 Great Bend Turnpike
Honesdale, Pennsylvania 18431

570-448-2904
elizal@msn.com
www.fineartquilts.com

Kathie Briggs

Showy Pink Lady Slippers | 13595 Phelps Road
© 2009 | Charlevoix, Michigan 49720
20" x 24" |
51 cm x 61 cm | 231-547-4971
| kathie@kathiebriggs.com
Nature | www.kathiebriggs.com

Jack Brockette

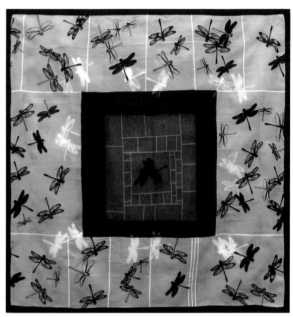

Front

Back

Swarming Dragonflies
© 2008
48" x 50"
122 cm x 127 cm

Conceptual

7358 Fieldgate Drive
Dallas, Texas 75230

214-365-0692
jack@brockette.com

Peggy A. Brown

Another Form
© 2009
42" x 52"
107 cm x 132 cm

Abstract

1541 Clay Lick Road
Nashville, Indiana 47448

812-988-7271
jpwestbreeze@aol.com
www.peggybrownart.com

Shelley Brucar

A Room With a View
© 2009
40" x 50"
102 cm x 127 cm

Nature

1399 Larchmont Drive
Buffalo Grove, Illinois 60089

847-921-4364
shelley@handmade-memories.com
www.handmade-memories.com

Betty Busby

Ending/Beginning | 14306 Oakwood Place
© 2009 | Albuquerque, New Mexico 87123
48" x 32" |
122 cm x 81 cm | 505-275-9511
| fbusby3@comcast.net
Figurative | www.bbusbyarts.com

Judith C. Busby

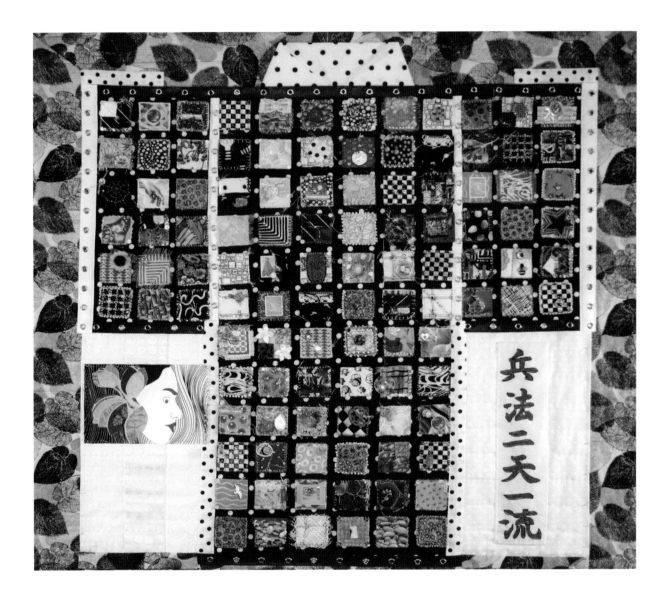

兵法二天一流

Hyoho Niten Ichi Ryu
© 2009
29" x 30"
75 cm x 76 cm

Conceptual

5928 Pocol Drive
Clifton, Virginia 20124

703-815-9093
judithcbusby@cox.net
www.judybusby.com

Leslie C. Carabas

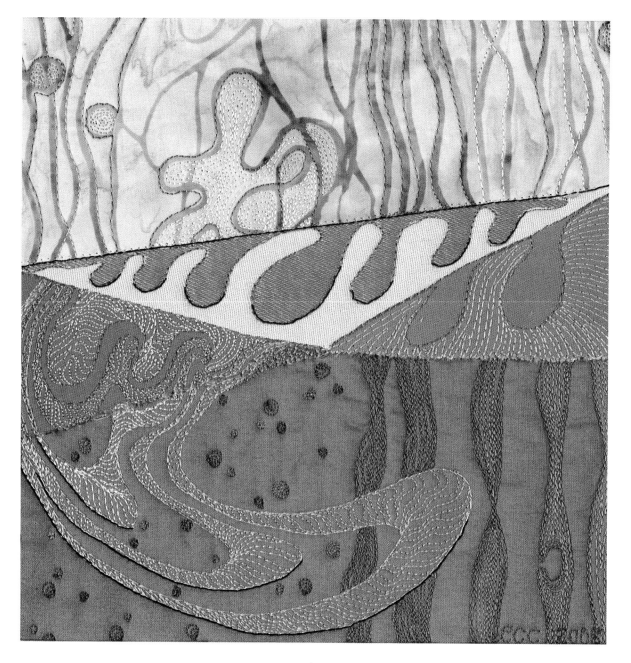

8 x 8, #2, 2008　　　　22686 Meadow Lane
© 2008　　　　Sonora, California 95370
8" x 8"
20 cm x 20 cm　　　209-532-0653
　　　　　　　　leslie@carabas.org
Abstract　　　www.leslie.carabas.org

Ruth G. Carden

Burning Bush | 1227 Manucy Road
© 2009 | Fernandina Beach, Florida 32034
30" x 22" |
76 cm x 56 cm | 904-277-1562
| rdcarden@gmail.com
Nature |

Lisa M. Chipetine

Private Lives
© 2008
26" x 38"
66 cm x 97 cm

Abstract

707 Maple Place
West Hempstead, New York 11552

516-857-3228
lisa@threadplay.com
www.threadplay.com

Paula Chung

Aging Iris 5
© 2009
80" x 53"
203 cm x 135 cm

Nature

P.O. Box 338
Zephyr Cove, Nevada 89448

775-588-3865
paula@paulachung.com
www.paulachung.com

Rosemary Claus-Gray

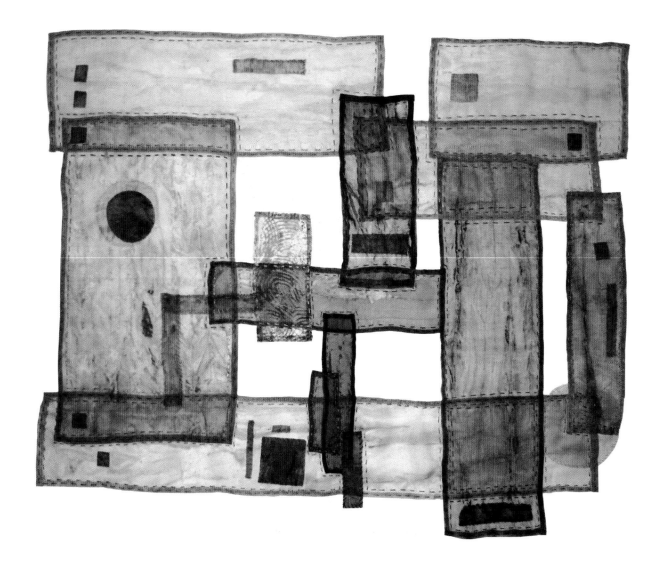

Balance | Route 1, Box 1605
© 2009 | Doniphan, Missouri 63935
30" x 36"
76 cm x 91 cm | 573-354-2634
| rosemary@semo.net
Abstract | www.rosemaryclaus-gray.com

Jette Clover

Letter Landscape 13
© 2008
40" x 40"
102 cm x 102 cm

Conceptual

Generaal van Merlenstraat 9
Antwerpen-Berchem, 02600
Belgium

+32 3 239 7437
jette@jetteclover.com
www.jetteclover.com

Martha Cole

Scots PIne | Box 42, RR#1
© 2009 | Lumsden, Saskatchewan S0G 3C0
48" x 48" | Canada
122 cm x 122 cm |
| 306-731-3298
Nature | mcole@sasktel.net
| www.marthacole.ca

Linda Colsh

White Widow
© 2009
40" x 40"
102 cm x 102 cm

Figurative

PSC 81 Box 51   or   Sijsjeslaan 32
APO, AE 09724   B-3078 Everberg
USA   Belgium

011-32-2-757-2580
linda@lindacolsh.com
www.lindacolsh.com

Joanell Connolly

It Took A Village | 6171 Sydney Drive
© 2009 | Huntington Beach, California 92647
17" x 17" |
43 cm x 43 cm | 714-893-4352
| joanell@joanell.com
Abstract | www.joanell.com

Jennifer Conrad

Flash Forward
© 2009
35" x 30"
89 cm x 78 cm

Abstract

765 Hampden Avenue, #206
St. Paul, Minnesota 55114

443-225-6740
jconrad@designsbyjconrad.com
www.designsbyjconrad.com

Judith Content

Mistral
© 2008
8" x 12"
20 cm x 31 cm

Abstract

827 Matadero Avenue
Palo Alto, California 94306

650-857-0289
judithcontent@earthlink.net

Nancy G. Cook

Late Summer Dawn
© 2009
24" x 37"
61 cm x 94 cm

Nature

6501 Brookfield Place
Charlotte, North Carolina 28270

704-366-9643
ngcook1@bellsouth.net
www.nancygcook.com

Jean McLaughlin Cowie

Juniper at Dawn
© 2009
46" x 32"
117 cm x 81 cm

Nature

29 Buffalo Bur Road
Silver City, New Mexico 88022

575-937-5843
jean@paintedrockquiltdesign.com
www.paintedrockquiltdesign.com

Robin C. Cowley

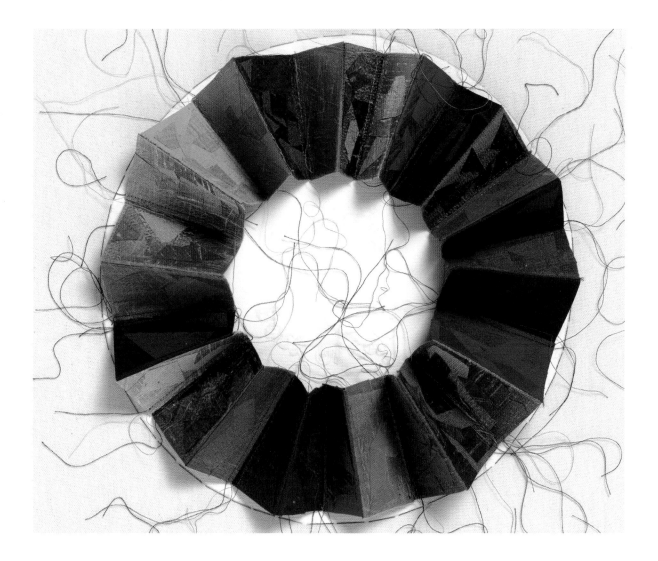

In Sight: Book of Colors
© 2008
12" x 12"
31 cm x 31 cm

Color Work

2451 Potomac Street
Oakland, California 94602

510-530-1134
art@RobinCowley.com
www.RobinCowley.com

Dena D. Crain

The Eyes Have it
© 2008
28" x 36"
71 cm x 91 cm

Conceptual

P.O. Box 1141
Nakuru, 20100
Kenya

+254-733-782147
dena@denacrain.com
www.denacrain.com

Denise A. Currier

Flowering Cereus II, Botanical Series
© 2008
13" x 16"
33 cm x 41 cm

Nature

8733 E. Russell Street
Mesa, Arizona 85207

480-964-6019
DeniseACurrier@msn.com
www.DeniseACurrier.com

Margaret Cusack

Telling Our Stories
© 2009
7" x 6"
18 cm x 15 cm

Figurative

124 Hoyt Street
Brooklyn, New York 11217

718-237-0145
cusackart@aol.com
www.MargaretCusack.com

Judy B. Dales

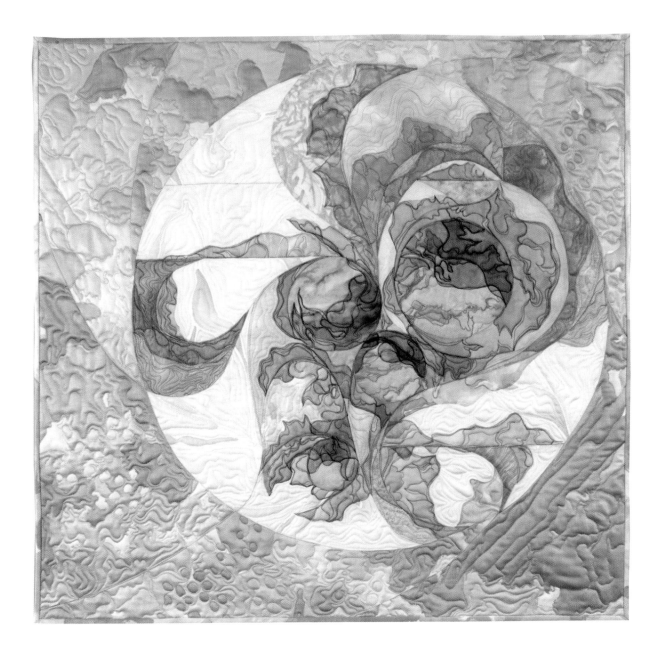

Moon Dreams
© 2009
35" x 36"
89 cm x 91 cm

Abstract

2254 Craftsbury Road
Greensboro, Vermont 05841

802-533-7733
judy@judydales.com
www.judydales.com

Yael David-Cohen

Pink Window
© 2008
19" x 16"
49 cm x 40 cm

Abstract

175 West Heath Road
London, NW3 7TT
United Kingdom

44 2084 587988
mail@simonyael.co.uk
www.yaeldc.co.uk

Fenella Davies

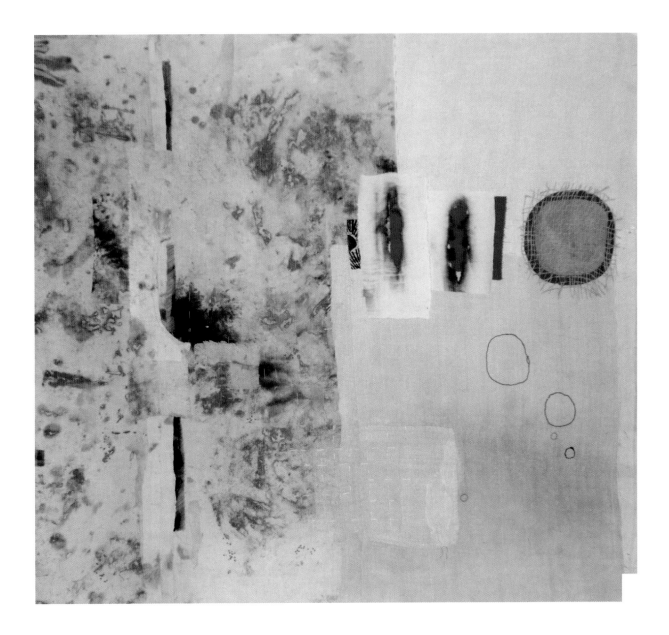

Venetian Fire
© 2008
39" x 41"
99 cm x 104 cm

Abstract

P.O. Box 1854
Bath, N. Somerset BA1 5XE
United Kingdom

0044(0)1225 333088
fenelladavies@btinternet.com
www.fenelladavies.com

Anna M. Davison

In My Garden Series: #1 Poppies
© 2009
32" x 20"
81 cm x 51 cm

Representational

186 Clearway Street
Mahone Bay, Nova Scotia B0J 2E0
Canada

902-624-9575
annadavison@eastlink.ca
www.AnnaQuilts.com

Sue Dennis

Anthills - Study in Gold
© 2008
31" x 30"
79 cm x 76 cm

Nature

31 Shelley Street, Sunnybank
Brisbane, Queensland 4109
Australia

+61 7 33454994
bsdennis@bigpond.com
www.suedennis.com

Segolene Diamant-Berger

Out of Depression | 6 route de la Saint Gilles
© 2008 | Cornille-les-Caves 49140
68" x 58" | France
175 cm x 148 cm |
 | +33 2 41 54 10 86
Abstract | segoquilt@dbnco.fr

Dianne V. Dockery

Canyon Crossing | 83 Boy Scout Road
© 2009 | Kutztown, Pennsylvania 19530
17" x 22"
43 cm x 56 cm | 610-683-6137
| dvdathome@yahoo.com
Abstract | www.diannevotterodockery.com

Pat Dolan

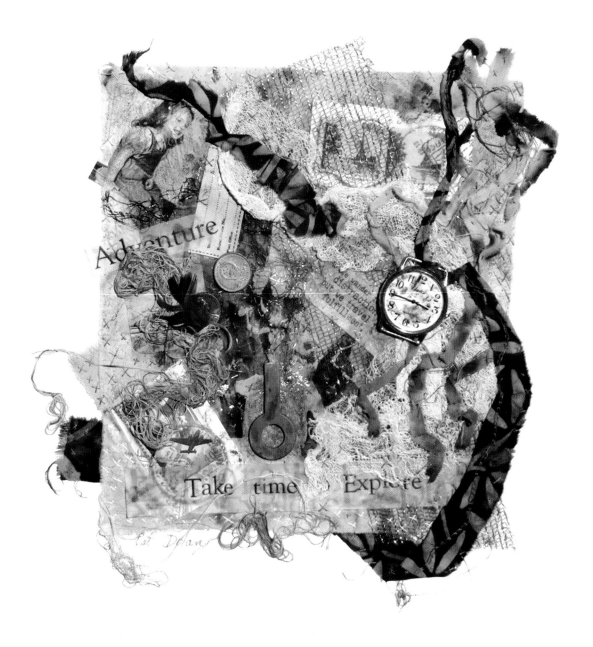

Rustine's Adventure
© 2008
16" x 16"
41 cm x 41 cm

Conceptual

1108 Mayberry Lane
State College, Pennsylvania 16801

814-308-8287
pat.dolan.artist@gmail.com
www.pat-dolan.com

Chiaki Dosho

Garret
© 2009
39" x 39"
100 cm x 100 cm

Conceptual

4-1-1-221, Hakusan, Asao-Ku
Kawasaki-Shi, Kanagawa-Ken 215-0014
Japan

+81-44-987-9120
chiakidoshoart@mac.com
web.mac.com/chiakidoshoart/

Eileen Doughty

The Alarm Clock Rings | 9701 Rhapsody Drive
© 2008 | Vienna, Virginia 22181
48" x 64" |
122 cm x 163 cm | 703-938-6916
| artist@DoughtyDesigns.com
Nature | www.DoughtyDesigns.com

Pat Durbin

Beside the Still Waters
© 2008
44" x 88"
112 cm x 224 cm

Nature

6265 Eggert Road
Eureka, California 95503

707-443-2047
stitching@suddenlink.net
www.patdurbin.com

Ginny Eckley

Gated Community VIII
© 2009
40" x 40"
102 cm x 102 cm

Nature

2423 Kings Forest Drive
Kingwood, Texas 77339

281-358-2951
ginny@mail.com
www.fabricpainting.com

Susan Else

Nothing to Fear
© 2008
49" x 30"
125 cm x 76 cm

Sculptural

126 Escalona Drive
Santa Cruz, California 95060

831-423-0515
selse@pacbell.net
www.susanelse.com

Noriko Endo

Lakeside Solace
© 2009
58" x 58"
148 cm x 149 cm

Nature

7-12-8 Kami-Soshigaya
Tokyo, 157-0065
Japan

81-3-3308-3800
norikoendojp@yahoo.co.jp
www.norikoendo.com

Wendy Feldberg

Garden Cloth 1
© 2009
48" x 16"
122 cm x 41 cm

Abstract

20 Wilton Crescent
Ottawa, Ontario K1S 2T5
Canada

613-232-1829
wendy.feldberg@sympatico.ca
www.wendyfeldberg.ca

Deborah Fell

Serendipity Duet 3
© 2008
42" x 62"
107 cm x 158 cm

Abstract

1412 Raintree Woods
Urbana, Illinois 61802

217-384-0544
deborahfell@comcast.net
www.deborahfell.com

Clairan Ferrono

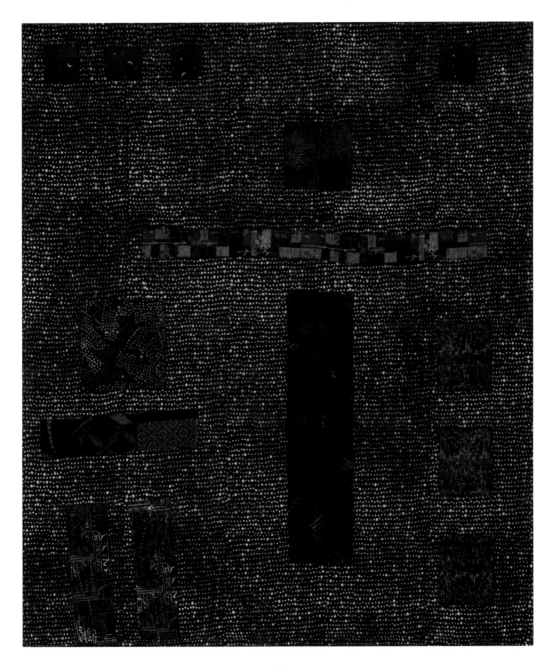

The Darkness Surrounds Us
© 2009
41" x 35"
103 cm x 88 cm

Conceptual

5432 S. Dorchester Avenue
Chicago, Illinois 60615

773-667-4403
fabric8tions@hotmail.com
www.clairanferrono.com

Linda Filby-Fisher

Unity 3, Medicine Wheel Series
© 2009
30" x 20"
76 cm x 51 cm

Conceptual

6401 W. 67th Street
Overland Park, Kansas 66202

913-722-1589
lffkc@yahoo.com
www.kansasartquilters.org

Jamie Fingal

Women Friends | 1500 E. Katella Avenue
© 2009 | Orange, California 92867
14" x 43" |
36 cm x 109 cm | 714-612-4621
               | jamie.fingal@gmail.com
Figurative | JamieFingalDesigns.blogspot.com/

Tommy Fitzsimmons

12 Tunes
© 2009
40" x 36"
102 cm x 91 cm

Abstract

642 Forestwood Drive
Romeoville, Illinois 60446

630-319-7553
tommygirl@americanstair.net
www.tommysartquilts.com

Floris Flam

Altered Perspectives 7
© 2009
14" x 16"
36 cm x 41 cm

Abstract

5450 Whitley Park Terrace, Apt. 104
Bethesda, Maryland 20814

301-530-7773
floris@florisflam.com
www.florisflam.com

Barb Forrister

Generation Y: Song of Hope
© 2009
50" x 46"
126 cm x 116 cm

Nature

4012 Tecate Trail
Austin, Texas 78739

512-672-9014
bjforrister@sbcglobal.net
www.freespiritartstudio.blogspot.com

Karin Franzen

Front

Back

Ecology of Fireweed
© 2009
44" x 44"
112 cm x 112 cm

Nature

388 Reynolds Lane
Fairbanks, Alaska 99712

907-488-7641
kfranzen@att.net
www.karinfranzen.com

Linda Frost

Geode Slices
© 2009
74" x 56"
188 cm x 142 cm

Abstract

1313 Raintree Place
Lawrence, Kansas 66044

785-841-3244
LLFrost@Sunflower.com
www.13thstreetstudio.com

Debra A. Gabel

It's a NEW Day!
© 2009
54" x 51"
137 cm x 130 cm

Figurative

13618 Meadow Glenn
Clarksville, Maryland 21029

410-531-9047
debra@zebrapatterns.com
www.zebrapatterns.com

Linda Gass

Sanitary?
© 2009
30" x 30"
76 cm x 76 cm

Nature

P.O. Box 1406
Los Altos, California 94023

650-948-1752
linda@lindagass.com
www.lindagass.com

Marilyn Gillis

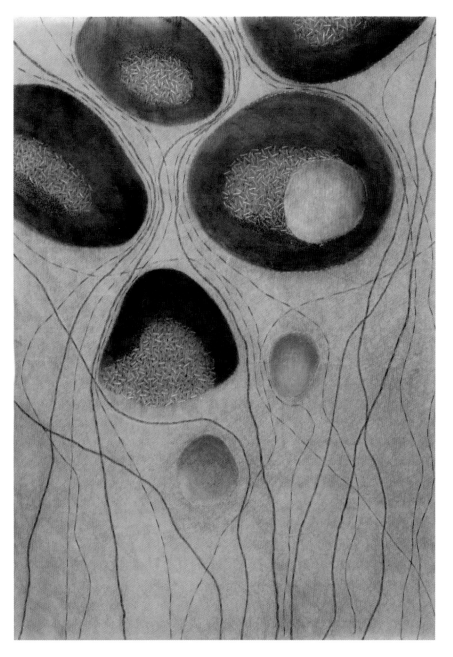

Inner Voice 1
© 2008
36" x 24"
91 cm x 61 cm

Abstract

6623 Spear Street
Shelburne, Vermont 05482

802-985-1415
marilyngillis@gmail.com

Rayna Gillman

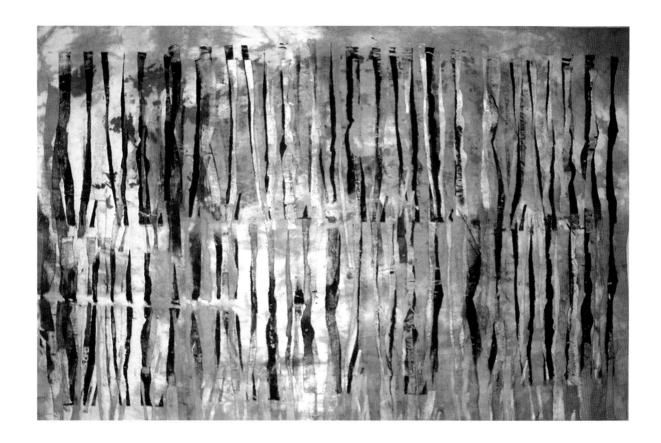

Element
© 2009
26" x 40"
65 cm x 102 cm

Abstract

78 Sullivan Drive
West Orange, New Jersey 07052

973-243-9443
rgillman@studio78.net
www.studio78.net

Karen Goetzinger

Abundance
© 2009
44" x 16"
112 cm x 41 cm

Abstract

5 Belgrave Road
Ottawa, Ontario K1S 0L9
Canada

613-231-4894
quiltopia@sympatico.ca
www.karengoetzinger.com

Jo-Ann Golenia

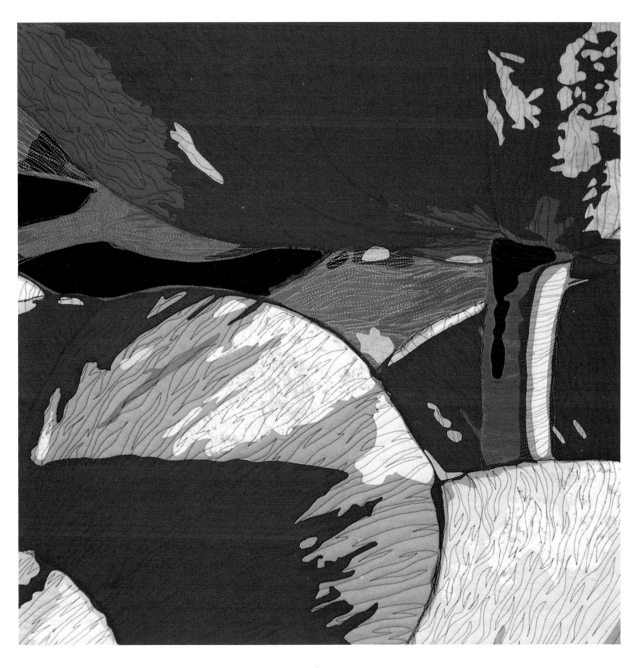

Tulips I
© 2009
24" x 24"
61 cm x 61 cm

Representational

P.O. Box 726
Venice, Florida 34284

941-497-5354
mail@Jo-AnnGolenia.com
www.Jo-AnnGolenia.com

Valerie S. Goodwin

Lay of the Land II | 1700 Kathryn Drive
© 2009 | Tallahassee, Florida 32308
54" x 84" |
137 cm x 213 cm | 850-878-9923
| valeriegoodwin@comcast.net
Nature | www.quiltsbyvalerie.com

Patricia Gould

Coastal Symphony
© 2009
51" x 37"
129 cm x 94 cm

Nature

12620 Towner Avenue N.E.
Albuquerque, New Mexico 87112

505-670-6364
patriciagould@msn.com
www.angelfiredesigns.com

Sandy Gregg

Galaxies
© 2009
34" x 29"
86 cm x 74 cm

Abstract

16 Watson Street
Cambridge, Massachusetts 02139

617-864-1890
sgregg55@doolan.net
www.sandygregg.com

Deborah Gregory

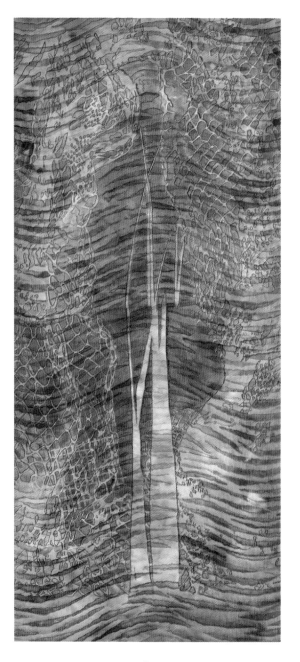

Choices and Pathways XII
© 2009
37" x 18"
94 cm x 46 cm

Abstract

12509 S.E. 19th Street
Bellevue, Washington 98005

425-746-8718
debkgreg@gmail.com
www.deborah-gregory.com

Cindy Grisdela

Salsa
© 2008
30" x 25"
76 cm x 64 cm

Color Work

708 Seneca Road
Great Falls, Virginia 22066

703-402-3116
cpgrisdela@gmail.com
www.cindygrisdela.com

Cara Gulati

Exploding Timelines
© 2009
68" x 54"
173 cm x 137 cm

Color Work

P.O. Box 6640
San Rafael, California 94903

415-662-2121
Cara@doodlepress.com
www.doodlepress.com

Gloria Hansen

Circles Collide
© 2009
50" x 42"
127 cm x 105 cm

Abstract

89 Oak Creek Road
East Windsor, New Jersey 08520

609-448-7818
gloria@gloderworks.com
www.gloriahansen.com

Tove Pirajá Hansen

Love Song
© 2009
20" x 16"
50 cm x 40 cm

Sculptural

Mattrupvej 4
Klovborg, DK 8765
Denmark

+45 98904147
tovinha@yahoo.com
www.tovepirajahansen.com

Michele Hardy

Circles #27: Rouge
© 2008
35" x 35"
89 cm x 89 cm

Abstract

6523 Tapadero Place
Castle Rock, Colorado 80108

303-663-2308
mhardy@michelehardy.com
www.michelehardy.com

Phillida Hargreaves

"The woods are lovely dark and deep"
© 2009
36" x 19"
91 cm x 48 cm

Nature

4060 Bath Road
Kingston, Ontario K7M 4Y4
Canada

613-389-8993
hargreavescp@sympatico.ca
www.phillidahargreaves.ca

Lynne G. Harrill

Heat Waves XIV: Reflections
© 2009
27" x 46"
69 cm x 117 cm

Color Work

105 Rae's Creek Drive
Greenville, South Carolina 29609

864-292-8708
lgharrill@yahoo.com
www.southernhighlandguild.org/harrill/

Carole Harris

Rhythm-a-ning | 15 East Kirby Street, Apt 611
© 2009 | Detroit, Michigan 48202
56" x 49"
142 cm x 125 cm | 313-871-2982
| charris@charris-design.com
Color Work | www.charris-design.com

Barbara Oliver Hartman

A Complete Unknown
© 2008
45" x 45"
113 cm x 113 cm

Abstract

122 Red Oak Lane
Flower Mound, Texas 75028

972-724-1181
barbaraohartman@aol.com
www.barbaraoliverhartman.com

Ann Harwell

Elephant's Trunk Nebula
© 2009
52" x 50"
132 cm x 127 cm

Abstract

6805 Lake Myra Road
Wendell, North Carolina 27591

919-771-8132
annharwell@aol.com
www.annharwell.com

Trisha Hassler

Sometimes The Reflection Is Our Friend
© 2009
20" x 20"
51 cm x 51 cm

Abstract

416 N.W. 13th Avenue, #608
Portland, Oregon 97209

503-228-8338
trisha@hasslerstudio.com
www.trishahassler.com

Patty Hawkins

Skeletal Tree Patterns
© 2008
28" x 23"
71 cm x 58 cm

Nature

530 Hondius Circle
Estes Park, Colorado 80517

970-577-8042
hawknestpw@gmail.com
www.pattyhawkins.com

Jim Hay

The Water Dances
© 2009
94" x 92"
239 cm x 234 cm

Nature

380-8 Yabara
Misato Takasaki, Gunma 370-3107
Japan

011 81 27 360-7061
jmhay@mail.wind.ne.jp
www7.wind.ne.jp/jimhay/

Annie Helmericks-Louder

Sleeping with Cows
© 2008
79" x 57"
201 cm x 145 cm

Figurative

667 S.W. 51 Road
Warrensburg, Missouri 64093

660-441-1420
helmericks@mac.com
www.helmericks.com

Linda W. Henke

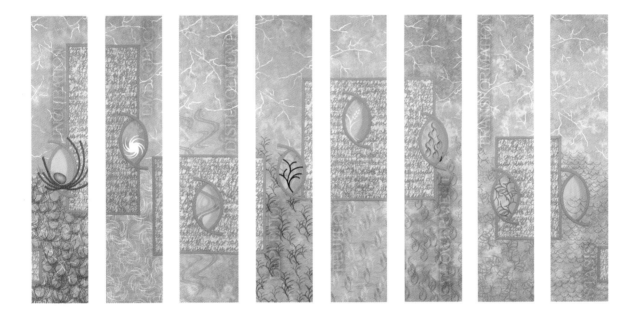

Tabula Rasa
© 2009
71" x 118"
180 cm x 300 cm

Conceptual

7139 Maple Bluff Lane
Indianapolis, Indiana 46236

317-826-0769
linda@lindahenke.com
www.lindahenke.com

Marilyn Henrion

Matidia | 505 LaGuardia Place #23D
© 2009 | New York, New York 10012
12" x 9" |
31 cm x 23 cm | 212-982-8949
| marilynhenrion@mac.com
Figurative | www.marilynhenrion.com

Anna Hergert

Glisten: Sunrise Over Buffalo Pound Lake
© 2008
68" x 23"
173 cm x 58 cm

Conceptual

P. O. Box 1274, Station Main
Moose Jaw, Saskatchewan S6H 4P9
Canada

306-692-8058
anna@annahergert.com
www.annahergert.com

Julie Hirota

Reflections | 3117 Mount Tamalpais Drive
© 2009 | Roseville, California 95747
12" x 12" |
31 cm x 31 cm | 916-412-4195
| julie@jhiro.com
Nature | www.jhiro.com

Sandra Hoefner

Waiting For Her Prince
© 2008
50" x 33"
127 cm x 84 cm

Figurative

2337 Meridian Court
Grand Junction, Colorado 81507

970-812-5680
shoefner2003@yahoo.com
www.sandrahoefner.com

Kristin Hoelscher-Schacker

Masquerade 3   1365 Neal Avenue North
© 2009   Lake Elmo, Minnesota 55042
29" x 29"
74 cm x 74 cm   651-436-6862
krishoel001@mac.com

Abstract

Rosemary Hoffenberg

Artichoke
© 2009
36" x 33"
91 cm x 84 cm

Abstract

89 Williams Street
Wrentham, Massachusetts 02093

508-384-3866
rozeeh@comcast.net
www.rosemaryhoffenberg.com

Sue Holdaway-Heys

Under The Canopy II
© 2009
44" x 36"
112 cm x 91 cm

Nature

2605 Powell Avenue
Ann Arbor, Michigan 48104

734-971-4980
shhart@aol.com
www.sueholdaway-heys.com

Cindi Huss

After the Storm II
© 2009
48" x 25"
122 cm x 64 cm

Nature

2117 Heatherly Road
Kingsport, Tennessee 37660

423-245-5408
cindi@cindihuss.com
www.cindihuss.com

Harumi Iida

Lost Bee | Yuigahama 2-8-13
© 2009 | Kamakura, 248-0014
37" x 26" | Japan
94 cm x 66 cm |
| +81-467-252593
Nature | hi_quilt@kamakuranet.ne.jp

Leslie Tucker Jenison

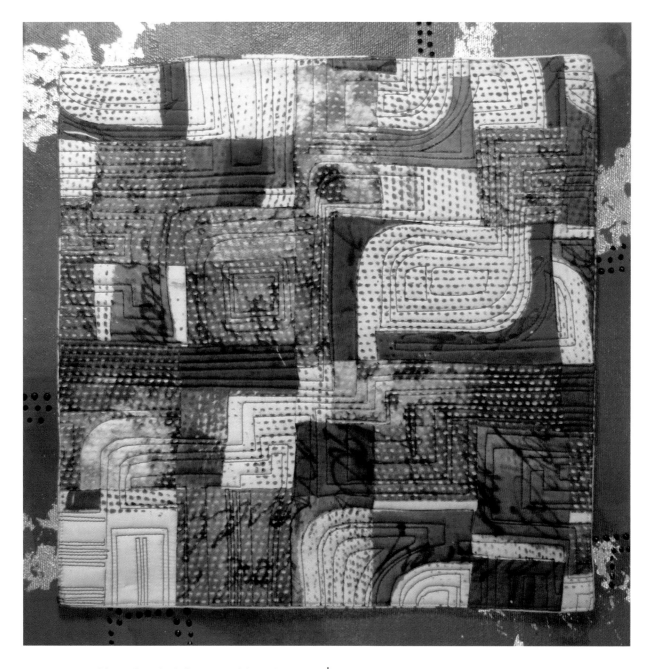

Heartland: A Personal Landscape
© 2009
12" x 12"
31 cm x 31 cm

Nature

104 Ponca Bend
San Antonio, Texas 78231

210-364-6067
leslie.jenison@gmail.com
leslietuckerjenison.blogspot.com/

Jill Jensen

Trio
© 2009
12" x 14"
31 cm x 36 cm

Nature

P.O. Box 1264
Forest, Virginia 24551

434-582-1237
jilljensenart@hotmail.com
www.jilljensenart.com

Marie Z. Johansen

Inflamed
© 2008
22" x 17"
56 cm x 43 cm

Conceptual

187 Westcott Drive
Friday Harbor, Washington 98250

360-378-5840
zquilts@centurytel.net
www.zquilts.com

Ann Johnston

Wave #9
© 2009
19" x 13"
48 cm x 33 cm

Abstract

2920 Upper Drive
Lake Oswego, Oregon 97035

503-635-6791
aj@annjohnston.net
www.annjohnston.net

Karen Kamenetzky

The Spaces Between V
© 2009
32" x 23"
80 cm x 58 cm

Abstract

448 Halladay Brook Road
Brattleboro, Vermont 05301

802-257-9156
kamburg@sover.net
www.karenkamenetzky.com

Kasia

Peace Pall
© 2009
80" x 36"
203 cm x 91 cm

Abstract

3215 Golf Road #227
Delafield, Wisconsin 53018

262-893-5510
Kasia@kasiasstudio.com
www.KasiasStudio.com

Peg Keeney

Reflections IV Bog | 7750 Bay Meadow Drive
© 2009 | Harbor Springs, Michigan 49740
36" x 38" |
91 cm x 97 cm | 231-409-2350
| keeney10@charter.net
Abstract | www.pegkeeney.com

Misik Kim

The Play 2
© 2009
55" x 55"
140 cm x 140 cm

Color Work

#102-201 Poonglim Iwant Apt
Seoul, 120-102
Korea

82-11-893-1963
Kmisik@naver.com

Catherine Kleeman

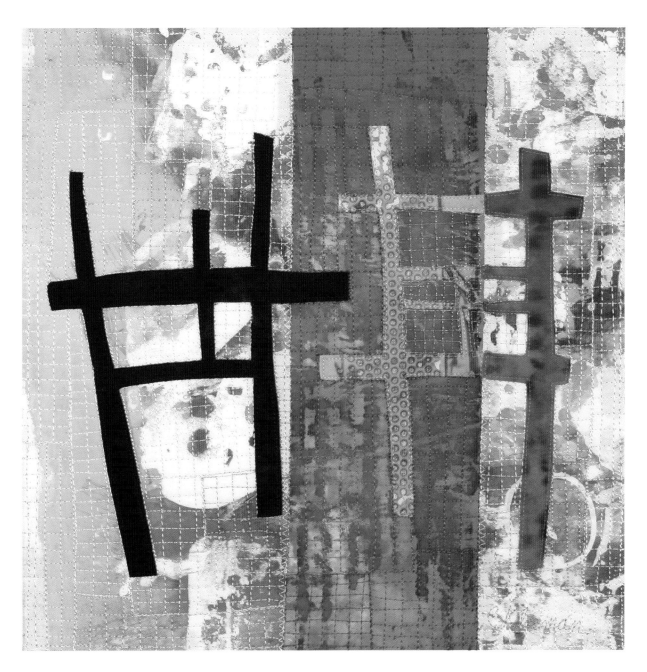

Ventanas 13
© 2008
12" x 12"
31 cm x 31 cm

Abstract

915 Army Road
Ruxton, Maryland 21204

410-321-9438
cathy@cathykleeman.com
www.cathykleeman.com

Sherry D. Kleinman

Date Night at the Drive In
© 2009
30" x 23"
76 cm x 58 cm

Figurative

17239 Avenida de la Herradura
Pacific Palisades, California 90272

310-459-4918
sherrykleinman@mac.com
www.sherrykleinman.com

Chris Kleppe

The Pumpkin Patch
© 2008
48" x 48"
122 cm x 122 cm

Color Work

110 North 80th Street
Milwaukee, Wisconsin 53213

414-476-3420
kleppe.milw@juno.com

Susan Brubaker Knapp

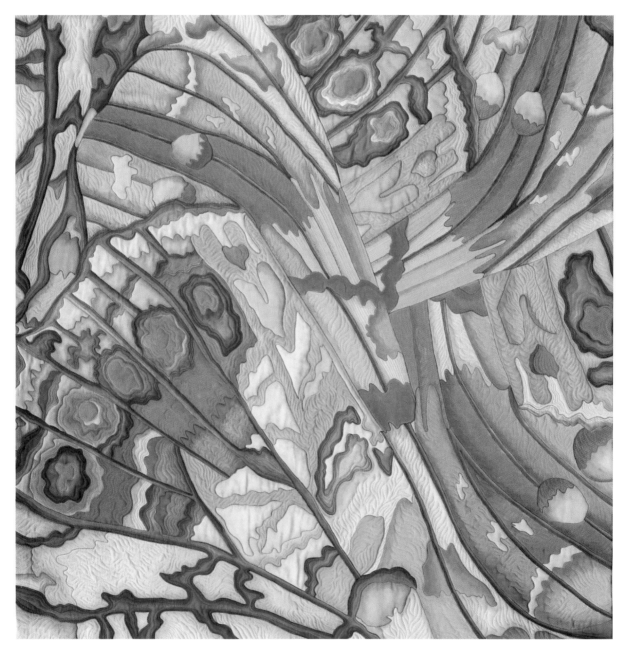

Lepidoptera
© 2009
39" x 39"
99 cm x 99 cm

Color Work

469 W. Center Avenue
Mooresville, North Carolina 28115

704-663-0335
susan@bluemoonriver.com
www.bluemoonriver.com

Terry Kramzar

Leaves
© 2009
40" x 40"
102 cm x 102 cm

Representational

702 Haldane Drive
Kennett Square, Pennsylvania 19348

610-388-8605
terry@terryKramzar.com
www.TerryKramzar.com

Pat Kroth

Inside Out | 2755 Hula Drive
© 2008 | Verona, Wisconsin 53593
56" x 42" |
142 cm x 107 cm | 608-845-3970
| krothp@juno.com
Abstract | www.krothfiberart.com

Marcia Ann Kuehl

Ice Cave
© 2009
13" x 19"
33 cm x 47 cm

Abstract

P. O. Box 7326
Capistrano Beach, California 92624

949-349-9311
ma.kuehl@gmail.com
www.polywog-fiberartstudio.com

Pat Kumicich

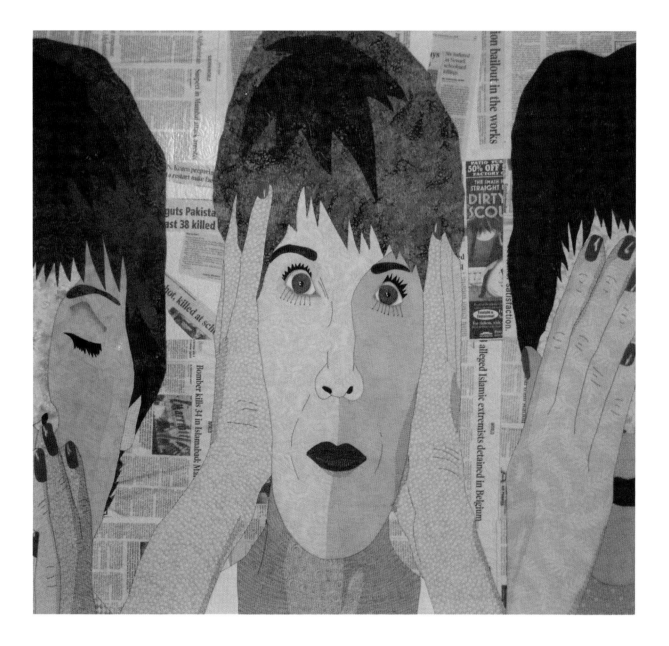

My Struggle
© 2009
50" x 49"
127 cm x 125 cm

Figurative

46 Newbury Place
Naples, Florida 34104

239-775-9517
patkumicich@me.com
www.patkumicich.com

Janet Kurjan

Migration
© 2009
37" x 33"
94 cm x 84 cm

Abstract

5400 N.E. 200th Place
Lake Forest Park, Washington 98155

206-367-0179
janet@janetkurjan.com
www.janetkurjan.com

Denise Labadie

Trinity Church
© 2009
45" x 38"
114 cm x 97 cm

Representational

819 Tempted Ways Drive
Longmont, Colorado 80504

303-682-9696
denise@labadiefiberart.com
www.LabadieFiberArt.com

Judy Langille

White Works II
© 2009
34" x 52"
86 cm x 132 cm

Abstract

1 Talcott Court
Kendall Park, New Jersey 08824

732-940-0821
judylangille7@gmail.com
www.judylangille.com

Kim M. LaPolla

Upon Another Winter's Day
© 2009
15" x 15"
38 cm x 38 cm

Nature

P.O. Box 659
Greenville, New York 12083

518-966-5219
klapolla@markim.com
www.CrazyByDesign.com

126

Carol Larson

Currents #8
© 2009
30" x 30"
76 cm x 76 cm

Abstract

7 Cader Court
Petaluma, California 94952

707-763-4525
cwlarson2@comcast.net
www.live2dye.com

Mary-Ellen Latino

Rhythm and Soul 3 | 23 Sears Road
© 2008 | Southborough, Massachusetts 01772
36" x 40"
91 cm x 102 cm | 508-904-0701
| melsrun2000@hotmail.com
Abstract

Sandra E. Lauterbach

"Pursonal" Passion
© 2009
36" x 28"
91 cm x 71 cm

Representational

539 Hanley Place
Los Angeles, California 90049

310-476-4849
sarogier@gmail.com
www.sandralauterbach.com

Eileen Lauterborn

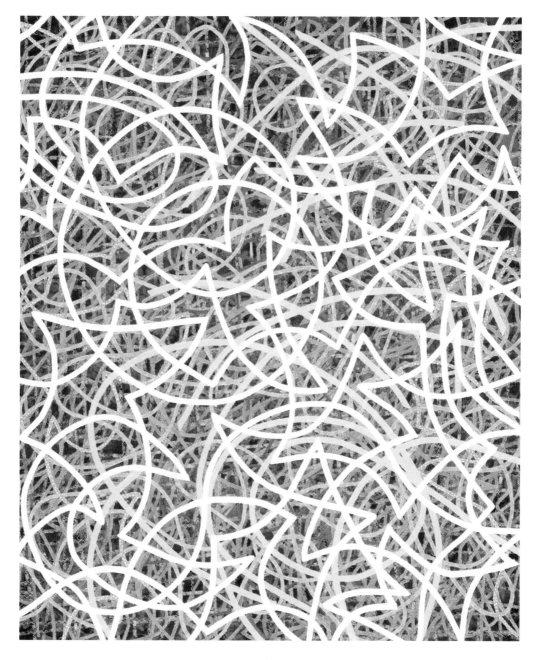

Afterimage
© 2009
41" x 34"
104 cm x 86 cm

Color Work

30 Frank Avenue
Farmingdale, New York 11735

516-694-2819
JGLandEFL@aol.com
www.eileenlauterborn.com

Catharina Breedyk Law

Madonna and Child #6
© 2009
39" x 27"
99 cm x 69 cm

Figurative

3045 Drummond Con.#2
Perth, Ontario K7H 3C3
Canada

613-267-7417
catelaw@ripnet.com

Linda Levin

City with Footnotes VIII | 10 Brewster Road
© 2008 | Wayland, Massachusetts 01778
49" x 40"
125 cm x 102 cm | 508-358-4248
| lindalevinart@gmail.com
Abstract | www.lindalevinart.com

Judy Zoelzer Levine

Passages
© 2008
47" x 31"
119 cm x 79 cm

Abstract

9415 N. Fairway Drive
Bayside, Wisconsin 53217

414-351-0325
judy@judylevine.com
judylevine.com

Hsin-Chen Lin

9F, No. 252, Sec. 2, Shulin St.
Tainan City, 700
Taiwan

+886-6-2149696
jenny.quilt@msa.hinet.net
www.linhsinchen.idv.tw

Joy
© 2009
34" x 49"
88 cm x 125 cm

Abstract

Ellen Lindner

Natural Progression | 3845 Peacock Drive
© 2009 | Melbourne, Florida 32904
24" x 38"
61 cm x 95 cm | 321-724-8012
| elindner@cfl.rr.com
Nature | www.adventurequilter.com

Karen Linduska

Glorious
© 2009
40" x 30"
102 cm x 76 cm

Nature

2523 Country Club Road
Carbondale, Illinois 62901

618-457-5228
linduskaartquilt@galaxycable.net
www.karenlinduska.com

Denise Linet

Memento | 11 Belmont Street
© 2009 | Brunswick, Maine 04011
37" x 36"
94 cm x 91 cm | 207-373-0331
dlinet@deniselinet.com
Abstract | www.DeniseLinet.com

Wendy Lugg

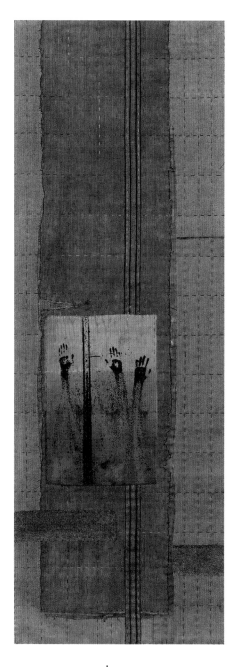

Mourning Cloth
© 2009
59" x 20"
150 cm x 50 cm

Abstract

20 Bass Road
Bull Creek, Western Australia 6149
Australia

61 8 9332 7075
wendy@wendylugg.com
www.wendylugg.com

Anne T. Lullie

Solar Flare I
© 2008
17" x 18"
43 cm x 46 cm

Abstract

1014 Burr Street
Lake in the Hills, Illinois 60156

847-658-2294
annelullie@gmail.com
www.annelullie.com

Susan L. Lumsden

Cypress Sunset
© 2008
56" x 42"
142 cm x 107 cm

Nature

221 N. 3rd Street
Thayer, Missouri 65791

417-274-1561
Susan@rebelquilter.com
www.rebelquilter.com

Kevan Lunney

Archeology: Genesis #7
© 2009
28" x 15"
71 cm x 38 cm

Abstract

18 Cherokee Road
East Brunswick, New Jersey 08816

732-723-0828
KevanartL@aol.com
www.KevanArt.com

Karin Lusnak

L'attitude bleu | 829 Stannage Avenue
© 2009 | Albany, California 94706
69" x 54" |
175 cm x 137 cm | 510-527-7294
| klusnak@cca.edu
Nature | www.KarinLusnak.com

Salley H. Mavor

Hush-a-bye-baby
© 2009
10" x 10"
25 cm x 25 cm

Figurative

11 Drumlin Road
Falmouth, Massachusetts 02540

508-540-1654
weefolk@cape.com
www.weefolkstudio.com

Therese May

Expression
© 2009
14" x 15"
37 cm x 38 cm

Figurative

1556 Wawona Drive
San Jose, California 95125

408-448-3247
therese@theresemay.com
www.theresemay.com

Kathleen McCabe

Protea
© 2009
31" x 41"
79 cm x 104 cm

Nature

250 H Avenue
Coronado, California 92118

619-435-1299
kathmccabe@gmail.com
www.kathleenmccabecoronado.com

Eleanor A. McCain

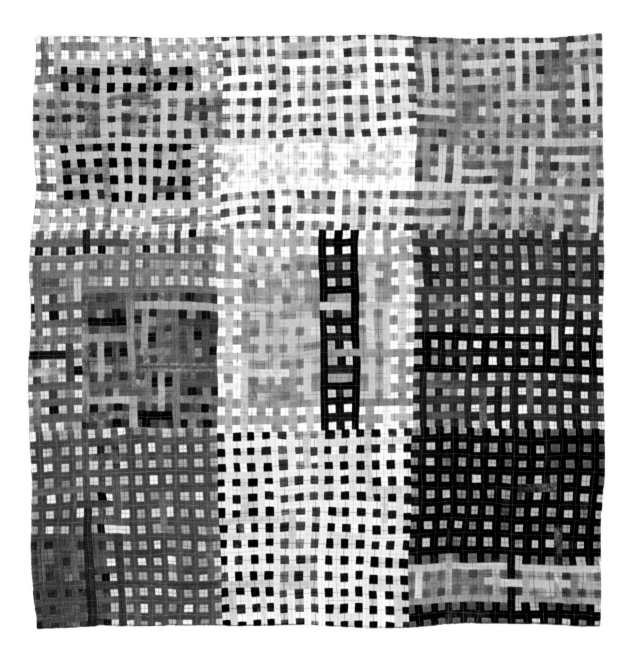

Green 2 | 87 Meigs Drive
© 2008 | Shalimar, Florida 32579
104" x 104" |
264 cm x 264 cm | 850-864-3815
| emccain@eleanormccain.net
Color Work | www.eleanormccain.net

Barbara McKie

Eye to Eye
© 2009
22" x 33"
56 cm x 84 cm

Nature

40 Bill Hill Road
Lyme, Connecticut 06371

860-434-5222
mckieart@comcast.net
www.mckieart.com

Salli McQuaid

Bad
© 2009
36" x 36"
91 cm x 91 cm

Figurative

216 Whistling Duck Road
Walla Walla, Washington 99362

509-876-4016
artistwriter@oplink.net
www.artistwriter.com

Libby & Jim Mijanovich

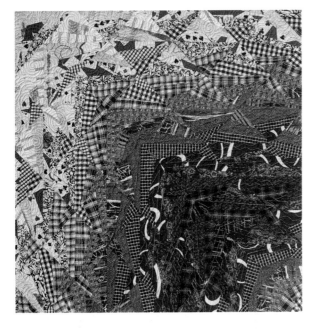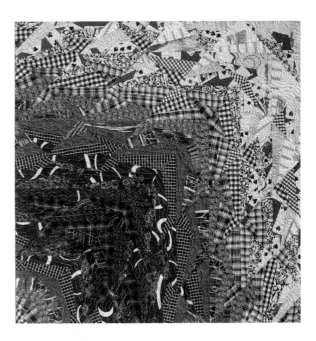
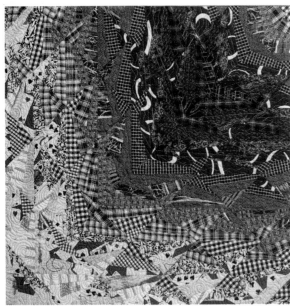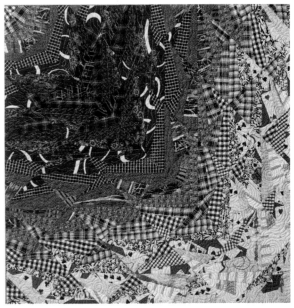

All In
© 2009
49" x 49"
125 cm x 125 cm

Abstract

651 Long Branch Road.
Marshall, North Carolina 28753

828-649-0200
contact@mijafiberart.com
www.mijafiberart.com

Karen I. Miller

Strata 2
© 2009
39" x 39"
99 cm x 98 cm

Nature

304 N.W. 28th Street
Corvallis, Oregon 97330

541-754-1573
karen@nautilus-fiberarts.com
www.nautilus-fiberarts.com

Dottie Moore

Om
© 2009
60" x 60"
152 cm x 152 cm

Conceptual

1134 Charlotte Avenue
Rock Hill, South Carolina 29732

803-327-5088
dottie@dottiemoore.com
www.dottiemoore.com

Lynne Morin

Mozart | 1 Hemlo Crescent
© 2009 | Kanata, Ontario K2T 1C7
26" x 29" | Canada
65 cm x 72 cm |
| 613-271-0946
Figurative | lynnemorin@rogers.com

Patti A. Morris

Alberta Rockies
© 2009
67" x 48"
170 cm x 122 cm

Nature

61 Allan Close
Red Deer, Alberta T4R 1A4
Canada

403-347-3247
p.tmorris@shaw.ca
www.morrisfabricartdesigns.com

Alison Muir

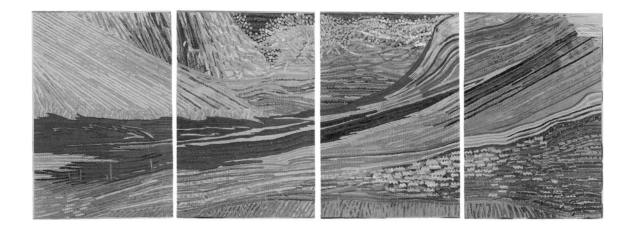

4 Year Term | Apt. 3, 40 Ben Boyd Road
© 2009 | Neutral Bay, New South Wales 2089
33" x 59" | Australia
85 cm x 150 cm |
| 61 411282010
Abstract | alison@muirandmuir.com.au

Ree Nancarrow

Mountains with Lupine Leaves
© 2009
26" x 27"
65 cm x 69 cm

Nature

P.O. Box 29
Denali Park, Alaska 99755

907-683-2376
reenan@mtaoline.net

Dominie M. Nash

Stills From a Life 36
© 2009
58" x 41"
147 cm x 104 cm

Still Life

8612 Rayburn Road
Bethesda, Maryland 20817

202-722-1407
dominien@verizon.net
www.dominienash.com

Sylvia J. Naylor

Fall in The Boreal Forest
© 2008
31" x 21"
79 cm x 53 cm

Nature

49 Scrimger Avenue
Cambridge, Ontario N1R 4V9
Canada

519-620-4503
sylvia.naylor@sympatico.ca
www.sylvianaylor.com

Stephanie Nordlin

Frazzled | 1672 Candlewick Drive S.W.
© 2009 | Poplar Grove, Illinois 61065
12" x 12"
31 cm x 31 cm | 815-260-0307
| snfashiony@yahoo.com
Representational | www.stephanienordlin.com

Dan Olfe

Celebration #2
© 2009
52" x 52"
132 cm x 132 cm

Color Work

P.O. Box 2106
Julian, California 92036

760-765-3219
danolfe@hotmail.com
www.danolfe.com

Pat Owoc

Return
© 2009
51" x 52"
130 cm x 132 cm

Nature

816 Bricken Place
St. Louis, Missouri 63122

314-821-7429
owocp@mindspring.com
www.patowoc.com

Mary B. Pal

Promise
© 2009
17" x 40"
45 cm x 102 cm

Nature

144 Broadway Avenue
Ottawa, Ontario K1S 2V8
Canada

613-567-2675
marybpal@gmail.com
www.MaryPalDesigns.com

B.J. Parady

Prairie Sunrise | 1154 Wintergreen Terrace
© 2009 | Batavia, Illinois 60510
11" x 23"
28 cm x 58 cm | 630-326-9316
info@bjparady.com
Abstract | www.bjparady.com

Bonnie Peterson

Valley of Domes
© 2008
43" x 45"
109 cm x 114 cm

Conceptual

22117 Royalwood Road
Houghton, Michigan 49931

630-673-5530
writebon@bonniepeterson.com
www.bonniepeterson.com

Mirjam Pet-Jacobs

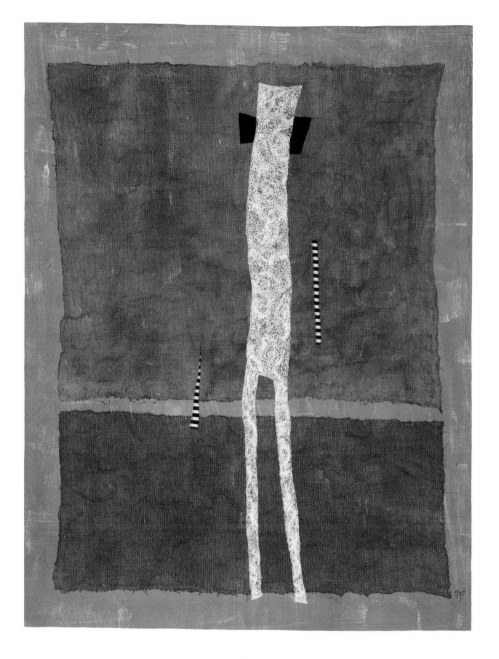

Floating Report | Rossinilaan 9
© 2008 | Waalre, NL-5583 ZC
68" x 52" | Netherlands
173 cm x 133 cm |
 | +31 40 221 7983
Abstract | mirjam@mirjampetjacobs.nl
 | www.mirjampetjacobs.nl

Julia E. Pfaff

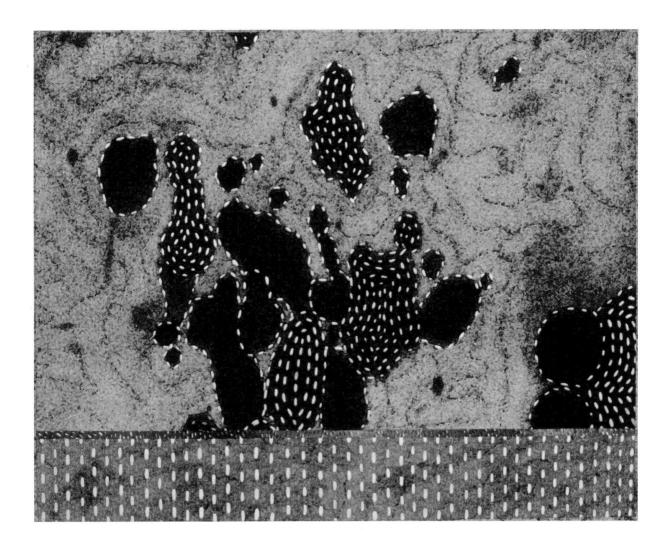

Contours III - Gravity
© 2008
34" x 40"
86 cm x 102 cm

Abstract

3104 Porter Street
Richmond, Virginia 23225

804-232-3966
jepfaff@aol.com

Pixeladies
Deb Cashatt and Kris Sazaki

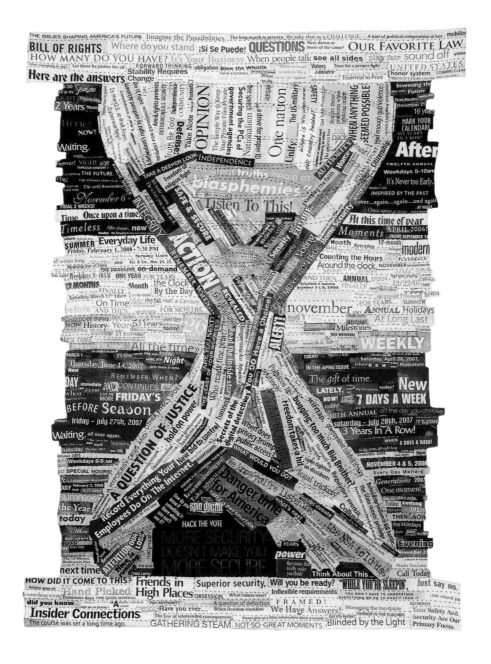

Just(ice) in Time?
© 2008
40" x 30"
102 cm x 76 cm

Conceptual

4061 Flying C Road
Cameron Park, California 95682

916-320-8774
info@pixeladies.com
www.pixeladies.com

Judith Plotner

Goddess Myth
© 2009
57" x 71"
144 cm x 180 cm

Conceptual

214 Goat Farm Road
Gloversville, New York 12078

518-725-3222
judith@judithplotner.com
www.judithplotner.com

Yvonne Porcella

Gigantus Interruptus | 3619 Shoemake Avenue
© 2009 | Modesto, California 95358
48" x 36"
122 cm x 91 cm | 209-795-1800
| yporcella@yahoo.com
Abstract | www.yvonneporcella.com

Casey Puetz

Abstract Study: Portals
© 2009
49" x 32"
125 cm x 81 cm

Abstract

515 S. Grandview Boulevard
Waukesha, Wisconsin 53188

262-549-0763
ppuetz@wi.rr.com
www.caseypuetz.com

Elaine M. Quehl

Standing Still
© 2008
29" x 21"
74 cm x 53 cm

Nature

1974 Gardenway Drive
Ottawa, Ontario K4A 3A2
Canada

613-824-8050
equehl@hotmail.com
www.equarelle.ca

Wen Redmond

Perception of Trees
© 2009
35" x 36"
89 cm x 91 cm

Abstract

441 First Crown Point Road
Strafford, New Hampshire 03884

603-332-8478
wenreddy@yahoo.com
www.wenredmond.com

Leslie Rego

Ancient Walls: Window to the Past
© 2008
45" x 31"
114 cm x 78 cm

Representational

P.O. Box 2358
Sun Valley, Idaho 83353

208-726-9100
quilt@LeslieRego.com
www.LeslieRego.com

Sue Reno

Fireball
© 2008
50" x 76"
127 cm x 193 cm

Nature

3824 Hillcrest Drive
Columbia, Pennsylvania 17512

717-371-0061
sue@suereno.com
www.suereno.com

Jan Rickman

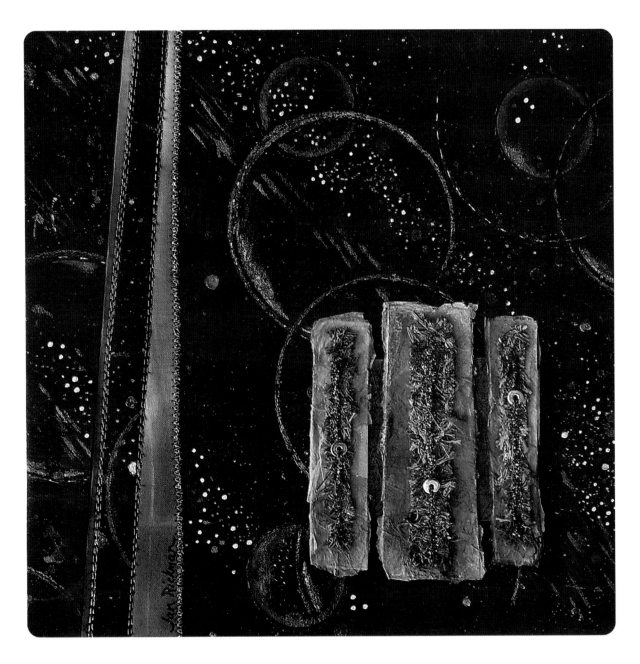

Galactic Synergy
© 2009
9" x 9"
23 cm x 23 cm

Abstract

P.O. Box 99
Whitewater, Colorado 81527

970-931-2231
janfantastic01@yahoo.com
www.janrickman.com

Connie Rohman

If Not Now, When?
© 2008
27" x 20"
69 cm x 51 cm

Conceptual

1031 W. Avenue 37
Los Angeles, California 90065

323-225-3321
crohman1@yahoo.com
www.connierohman.com

Rose Rushbrooke

Rabbit Hole | 6409 N. Orleans Avenue
© 2008 | Tampa, Florida 33604
16" x 13"
41 cm x 32 cm | 813-335-1634
| rose@roserushbrooke.com
Abstract | www.roserushbrooke.com

Carol Schepps

Summer Beaches
© 2008
33" x 49"
83 cm x 125 cm

Color Work

10 Marblehead Drive
Princeton Junction, New Jersey 08550

609-275-9440
carol@carolschepps.com
www.carolschepps.com

Norma Schlager

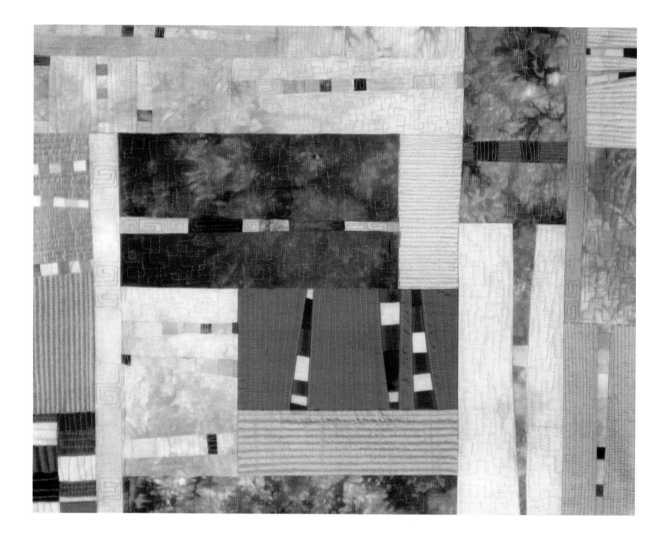

No Elephants Here
© 2009
18" x 24"
46 cm x 61 cm

Abstract

134 Logging Trail Road
Danbury, Connecticut 06811

203-798-0025
nschlager11@comcast.net
www.normaschlager.com

Maya Schonenberger

Yangtze 1
© 2008
20" x 20"
51 cm x 51 cm

Nature

8801 N.W. 189 Terrace
Miami, Florida 33018

305-829-7609
maya.schonenberger@gmail.com
www.mayaschonenberger.com

Karen M. Schulz

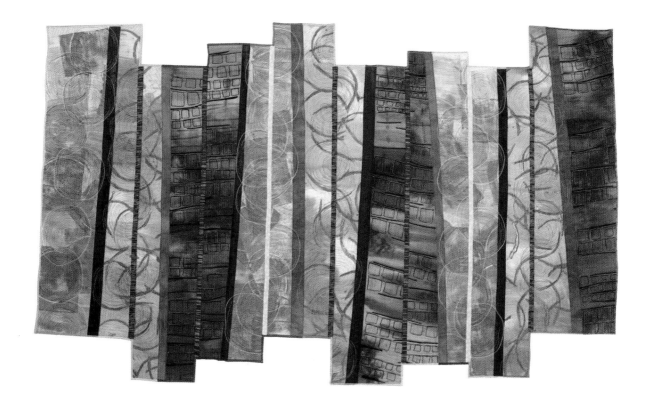

Round Peg/Square Hole
© 2009
32" x 54"
81 cm x 136 cm

Abstract

9204 Second Avenue
Silver Spring, Maryland 20910

301-588-0427
campbellk@starpower.net
www.karen-schulz.com

Alison M. Schwabe

Timetracks 11
© 2008
55" x 39"
140 cm x 100 cm

Abstract

Divina Comedia 2041
11500 Carrasco, Montevideo
Uruguay

+598 2600 0053
alison@alisonschwabe.com
www.alisonschwabe.com

Emmie Seaman

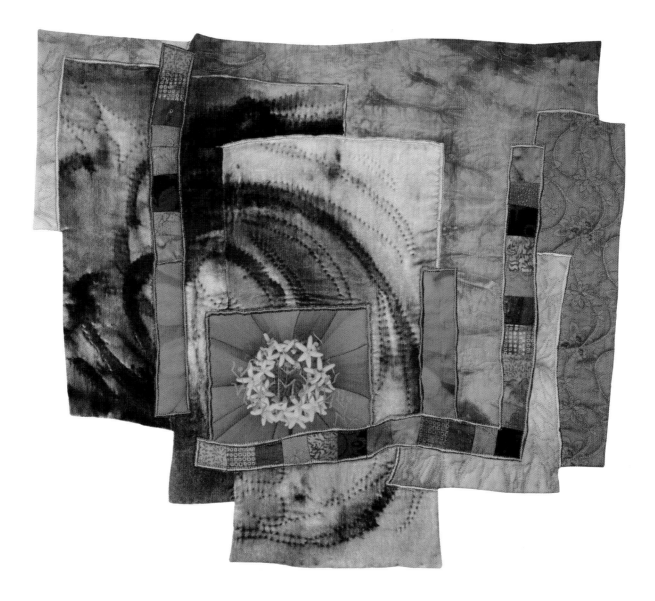

Zinnia | 14900 North Orleans Trail
© 2009 | Stockton, Missouri 65785
22" x 25" |
56 cm x 64 cm | 417-276-7794
| eseaman@windstream.net
Abstract | www.emmieseaman.com

Merle Axelrad Serlin

Sierra Water
© 2009
58" x 34"
147 cm x 86 cm

Nature

2600 14th Street
Sacramento, California 95818

916-442-0464
merleserlin@gmail.com
www.AxelradArt.com

Sandra Sider

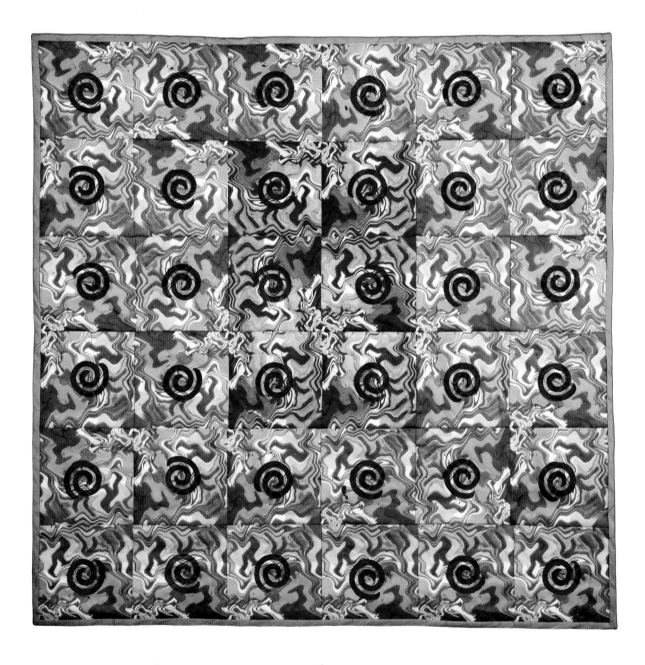

On the Road: Road Rage
© 2010
40" x 41"
100 cm x 103 cm

Conceptual

3811 Orloff Avenue
Bronx, New York 10463

718-390-7473
sandrasider@mac.com
www.sandrasider.com

Bonnie J. Smith

In Full Bloom
© 2009
48" x 69"
122 cm x 175 cm

Abstract

45 Devine Street
San Jose, California 95110

408-298-7898
bjs8934@aol.com
www.bonniejofiberarts.com

Lura Schwarz Smith

Angel of Roses
© 2009
35" x 32"
89 cm x 81 cm

Figurative

P.O. Box 649
Coarsegold, California 93614

559-683-6899
lura@lura-art.com
www.lura-art.com

Sarah Ann Smith

Naiads
© 2009
49" x 18"
125 cm x 46 cm

Figurative

17 Pleasant Ridge Drive
Camden, Maine 04843

207-236-6003
sarah@sarahannsmith.com
www.sarahannsmith.com

Joan Sowada

Yellow Trees | 206 W. Hogeye Drive
© 2009 | Gillette, Wyoming 82716
27" x 40" |
69 cm x 102 cm | 307-682-1657
| jsowada@vcn.com
Nature | www.avacenter.org

Marialuisa Sponga

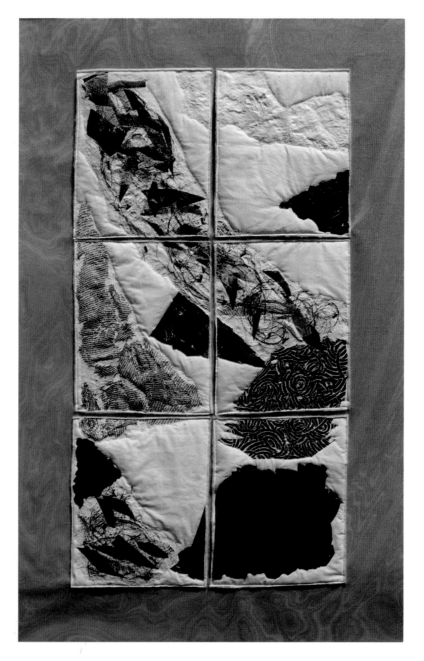

Wavering Landscape n.3
© 2008
73" x 47"
186 cm x 120 cm

Abstract

Località Olgiasca, n. 60
I-23823 Colico (Lecco)
Italy

0039 0341 931 932
gisponga@tin.it
www.sponga.com

Sue Spurlock

Long Winter's Nap
© 2009
9" x 10"
23 cm x 25 cm

Nature

1458 E. Gary Drive
Carbondale, Illinois 62902

618-529-3080
suespurlock@gmail.com
suespurlock.blogspot.com

Tracy McCabe Stewart

Midnight River
© 2009
35" x 72"
89 cm x 183 cm

Nature

251 Parker Drive
Grayslake, Illinois 60030

847-223-7032
tracy@mccabestewart.com
www.tracymccabestewart.com

Priscilla Stultz

Blooming
© 2008
29" x 30"
74 cm x 76 cm

Nature

3516 Cornell Road
Fairfax, Virginia 22030

703-591-5630
quilter73@hotmail.com
www.priscillastultz.com

Tiziana Tateo

Cover Girls
© 2009
40" x 63"
103 cm x 161 cm

Figurative

via Fratelli Cagnoni, 12
Vigevano, 27029
Italy

+39 0381 690617
vtateo@alice.it
www.tizianatateo.it

Carol Taylor

Moonglow
© 2008
53" x 35"
135 cm x 89 cm

Color Work

234 Railroad Mills Road
Pittsford, New York 14534

585-381-4425
ctquilts@rochester.rr.com
www.caroltaylorquilts.com

Daphne P. Taylor

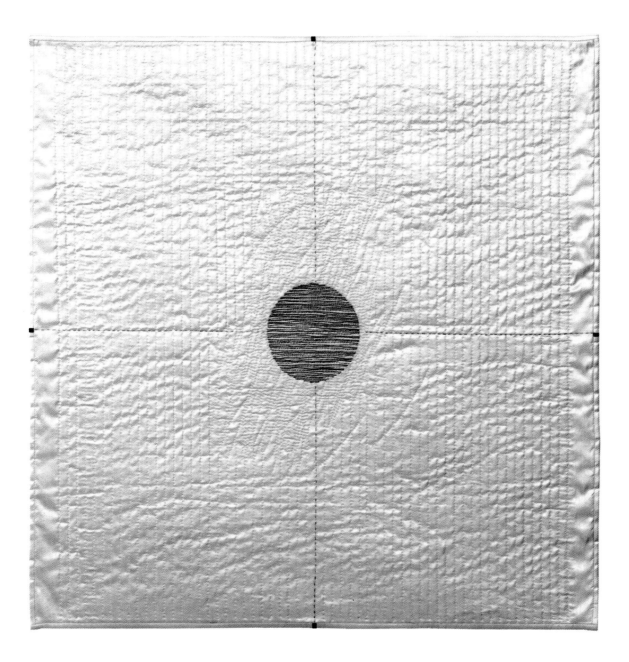

Quilt Drawing #12
© 2009
30" x 30"
75 cm x 75 cm

Abstract

40 Harrison Street, Apt. 34E
New York, New York 10013

212 -240-0281
daphnetaylorquilts@gmail.com
www.daphnetaylorquilts.com

Gwyned Trefethen

Botswana Bounty
© 2008
30" x 30"
76 cm x 76 cm

Conceptual

2953 Fox Run
Appleton, Wisconsin 54914

508-369-7595
gwynedtrefethen@mac.com
www.gwynedtrefethen.com

Janet Twinn

Gleam
© 2009
35" x 35"
89 cm x 89 cm

Abstract

11a, Tower Road
Tadworth, Surrey KT20 5QY
United Kingdom

+44 (0) 1737 812136
janet@jtwinn.freeserve.co.uk
www.janettwinn.co.uk

Ulva Ugerup

Angels of Wrath
© 2008
27" x 43"
70 cm x 110 cm

Figurative

Sparsnogatan 60
Lund, S 22652
Sweden

+46(0)46306601
ulva.ugerup@telia.com

Grietje van der Veen

Hibernation
© 2009
45" x 34"
115 cm x 86 cm

Nature

Hohestrasse 134
Oberwil, CH-4104
Switzerland

41614015655
grietje@textileart.ch
www.textileart.ch

Mary Vaneecke

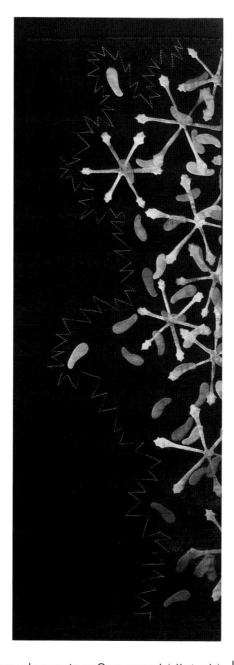

Complementary Samaras I (diptych)
© 2009
40" x 30"
102 cm x 76 cm

Abstract

2000 South Hermosa
Tucson, Arizona 85713

520-444-7149
mary@maryvaneecke.com
www.maryvaneecke.com

Desiree Vaughn

Approaching Storm
© 2009
26" x 33"
66 cm x 83 cm

Abstract

5900 S. Calle Court
Suttons Bay, Michigan 49682

231-409-2581
desiree@desireevaughn.com
www.desireevaughn.com

Terry Waldron

Papyrus
© 2009
45" x 25"
114 cm x 64 cm

Nature

6160 E. Morningview Drive
Anaheim, California 92807

714-921-1143
terryannwaldron@earthlink.net
www.terrywaldron.com

Nelda Warkentin

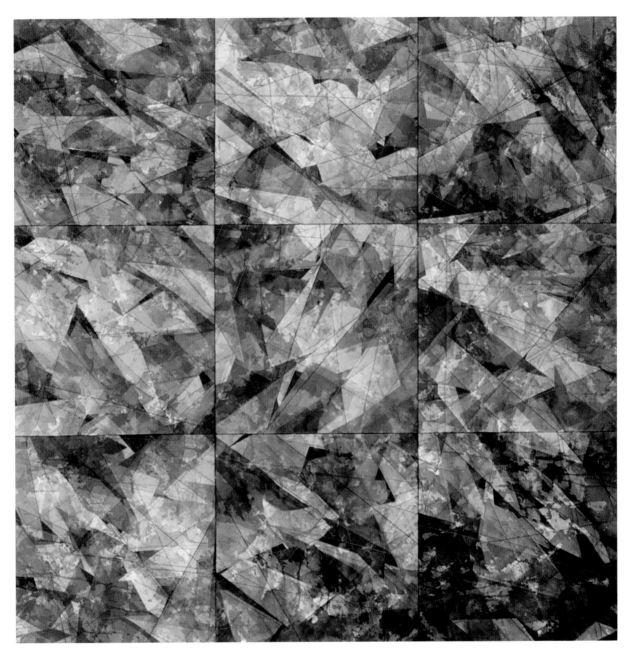

Sea Ice
© 2008
36" x 36"
91 cm x 91 cm

Color Work

1130 West 6th Avenue #7
Anchorage, Alaska 99501

907-279-0907
nelda.art@hotmail.com
www.neldawarkentin.com

Laura Wasilowski

Leafing Large
© 2009
41" x 42"
104 cm x 107 cm

Color Work

324 Vincent Place
Elgin, Illinois 60123

847-931-7684
laura@artfabrik.com
www.artfabrik.com

Carol Ann Waugh

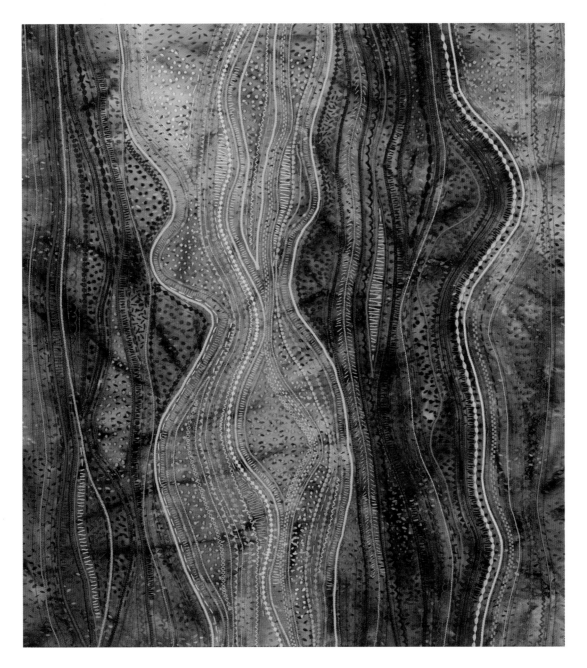

Celebrating Our Diversity | 1163 Vine Street
© 2009 | Denver, Colorado 80206
28" x 26" |
71 cm x 66 cm | 303-388-5215
| carol@carolannwaugh.com
Abstract | www.carolannwaugh.com

Kathy Weaver

Strategic Alliance
© 2008
48" x 56"
122 cm x 141 cm

Conceptual

2713 Port Clinton Road
Highland Park, Illinois 60035

847-432-0734
kweaverarts@comcast.net
www.kweaverarts.com

Deborah Weir

Seawall: Darwin, Australia
© 2009
27" x 33"
69 cm x 84 cm

Abstract

21 Encanto Drive
Rolling Hills Estates, California 90274

310-325-1895
FiberFly@cox.net
www.DeborahWeir.net

Barbara J. West

Windows to Nowhere
© 2009
19" x 20"
48 cm x 50 cm

Abstract

1020 9th Avenue
Canmore, Alberta T1W 1Z6
Canada

403-678-6500
barbarajwest@nucleus.com

Leni Levenson Wiener

Twilight Time
© 2009
22" x 19"
56 cm x 47 cm

Figurative

321 Beechmont Drive
New Rochelle, New York 10804

914-654-0366
Leni@leniwiener.com
www.leniwiener.com

Jayne E. Willoughby Scott

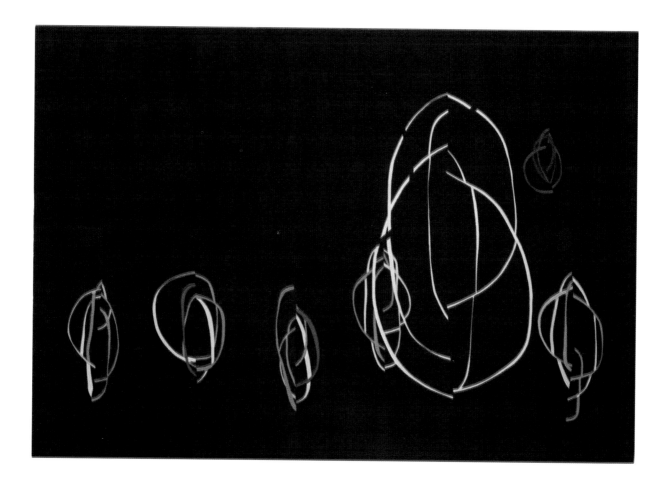

Night Drawing #2
© 2008
41" x 59"
104 cm x 149 cm

Abstract

9011 - 140 Street
Edmonton, Alberta T5R 0J4
Canada

780-437-7367
jws@incentre.net
www.jaynewilloughbyscott.com

Barb A. Wills

Layered Structures #100
© 2008
36" x 44"
91 cm x 112 cm

Abstract

1593 S. Oak Knoll Drive
Prescott, Arizona 86303

928-445-2796
wills.barb@yahoo.com
www.barbwills.com

Kathy York

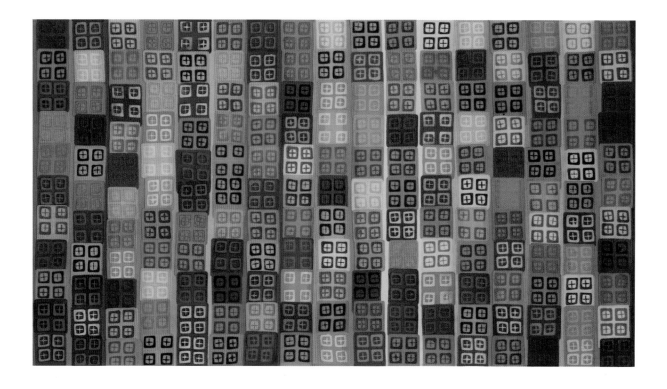

Building Up
© 2009
43" x 77"
109 cm x 196 cm

Color Work

4202 Hyridge Drive
Austin, Texas 78759

512-338-4271
kakiyork@gmail.com
www.aquamoonartquilts.blogspot.com

Charlotte Ziebarth

Reflection/Ripples View #1
© 2008
49" x 43"
125 cm x 109 cm

Abstract

3070 Ash Avenue
Boulder, Colorado 80305

303-494-2601
cziebarth@aol.com
www.charlotteziebarth.com

Alpha Index

Alpha Index continued

Geographic Index

Geographic Index *continued*

Geographic Index *continued*

Genre Index

Genre Index continued

Sponsors

Studio Art Quilt Associates, Inc. is supported by generous donations from individuals and organizations, including our Platinum Sponsors:

American Quilter's Society
www.americanquilter.com

Superior quality cotton threads for professional and domestic quilters
www.aurifil.com

www.Quilts.com

P.O. Box 572
Storrs, CT 06268-0572
USA
860-487-4199
www.SAQA.com ● info@SAQA.com